*This collection of joy
belongs to*

LAUGH AGAIN

CHARLES R. SWINDOLL

LAUGH AGAIN

Unless otherwise indicated, Scripture quotations used in this book are from the New American Standard Bible (NASB) © 1960, 1962, 1963, 1968, 1971, 1972, 1973, 1975, 1977 by the Lockman Foundation. Used by permission.

Library of Congress Cataloging-in-Publication Data

Swindoll, Charles R.
    Laugh again : experience outrageous joy / Charles R. Swindoll.
        p.   cm.
    Abridged ed. in minibook format.
    ISBN 0-8499-5027-9
    1. Joy—Religious aspects—Christianity.   2. Laughter—
Religious aspects—Christianity.   I. Title.
BV4647.J68S95   1993
248.4—dc20   93-19144
                                                           CIP

34569 PLP   9 8 7 6 5 4 3 2 1

Printed in Hong Kong

CHAPTER ONE

*T*his is a book about joy.

It's about relaxing more, releasing the tension, and refusing to let circumstances dominate our attitudes.

It's about looking at life from a perspective other than today's traffic report or the evening news.

It's about giving the child within us permission to look at life and laugh again.

Cynthia and I are into Harley-Davidson motorcycles.

I know, I know . . . it doesn't fit our image. What would ever possess me to start messing around with a motorcycle, cruising some of the picturesque roads down by the ocean, or taking off with my son for a relaxed, easygoing two or three hours together? What's this all about?

It's about forgetting all the nonsense that every single moment in life is serious. It's about breaking the thick and rigid mold of predictability. It's about enjoying a completely different slice of life where I don't have to concern myself with living up to anyone else's expectations or worry about who thinks what.

It's about being with one of our kids in a world that is totally on his turf (for a change), not mine, in a setting that is just plain fun, not work. It's about being me, nobody else.

It's about breaking the bondage of tunnel vision. It's about refusing to live my life playing one note on one instrument in one room and finding pleasure in a symphony of sounds and sights and smells. It's about widening the radius of a restrictive and demanding schedule where breathing fresh air is sometimes difficult and thinking creative thoughts is occasionally the next thing to impossible.

Bottom line, it's about freedom. That's it, plain and simple. It's about being free.

It's about entering into a tension-free, worry-free world where I don't have to say something profound or fix anyone or do anything other than feel the wind and smell the flowers and hug my wife and laugh till we're hoarse.

That's it in a nutshell. . . it's about freeing ourselves up to laugh again.

CHAPTER TWO

*Y*our Smile Increases Your Face Value

I know of no greater need today than the need for joy. Unexplainable, contagious joy. Outrageous joy.

The apostle Paul wrote several letters during his years of house arrest, one of which was addressed to a group of Christians living in Philippi. It is an amazing letter, made even more remarkable by its recurring theme—joy. Think of it! Written by a man who had known excruciating hardship and pain, living in a restricted setting chained to a Roman soldier, the letter to the Philippians resounds with joy!

Attitudes of joy and contentment are woven through the tapestry of these 104 verses like threads of silver. Rather than wallowing in self-pity or calling on his friends to help him escape or at least find relief from these restrictions, Paul sent a surprisingly lighthearted message.

As I attempt to find some secret clue to his joy, I have to conclude that it was his confidence in God. To Paul, God was in full control of everything. Everything!

If hardship came, God permitted it. If pain dogged his steps, it was only because God allowed it. If he was under arrest, God still remained the sovereign director of his life. If there seemed to be no way out, God knew he was pressed. If things broke open and all pressure was relieved, God was responsible.

My point? God is no distant deity but a constant reality, a very present help whenever needs occur. So? So live like it. And laugh like it! Paul did. While he lived, he drained every drop of joy out of every day that passed.

Basically there are two kinds of people: people who choose joy and people who don't. People who choose joy pay no attention to what day of the week it is . . . or how old they are . . . or what level of pain they are in. They have deliberately decided to laugh again because they have chosen joy.

People who do not choose joy miss the relief laughter can bring. And because they do not, they cannot. And because they can't they won't. Which one are you?

CHAPTER THREE

Regardless of How Severely the Winds of Adversity May Blow, Set Your Sails Toward Joy

There are Three Joy-Stealers: Worry . . . Stress . . . Fear. How do we withstand these joy stealers? Let me tell you what I do.

First I remind myself, "God, You are at work, and You are in control. And, Lord God, You know this is happening. You were there at the beginning, and You will bring everything that occurs to a conclusion that results in Your greater glory in the end." And then? Then (and only then!) I relax. From that point on, it really doesn't matter all that much what happens. It is in God's hands.

Nothing can rob you of your hold on grace, your claim to peace, or your confidence in God without your permission. Choose joy. Never release your grip!

I have lived almost fifty-eight years on this old earth, and I am more convinced than ever that the single most important choice a follower of Christ can make is his or her choice of attitude. Only you can determine that. Choose wisely . . . choose carefully . . . choose confidently.

Most people think that happiness is something that happens to them rather than something they deliberately and diligently pursue. Circumstances seldom generate smiles and laughter. Joy comes to those who determine to pursue it in spite of their circumstances.

These minds of ours are like bank vaults awaiting our deposits. If we regularly deposit positive, encouraging, and uplifting thoughts, what we withdraw will be the same. And the interest paid will be joy.

The secret of living is the same as the secret of joy: Both revolve around the centrality of Jesus Christ. In other words, the pursuit of happiness is the cultivation of a Christ-centered, Christ-controlled life.

When money is our objective, we must live in fear of losing it, which makes us paranoid and suspicious. When fame is our aim, we become competitive lest others upstage us, which makes us envious. When power and influence drive us, we become self-serving and strong-willed, which makes us arrogant.

And when possessions become our god, we become materialistic, thinking enough is never enough, which makes us greedy. All these pursuits fly in the face of contentment . . . and joy.

Let go. Let go of your habit of always looking at the negative. Let go of your need to fix everybody else's unhappiness. Let go of your drive to compete or compare. Let go of so many needless inhibitions that keep you from celebrating life. Quit being so protective . . . so predictable . . . so proper.

CHAPTER FOUR

*T*he Hidden Secret of a Happy Life

What is the most Christlike attitude on earth? Love? Patience? Grace?

As important as those traits may be, they are not the ones Jesus Himself referred to when He described Himself for the only time in Scripture:

"Come to Me, all who are weary and heavy-laden, and I will give you rest. Take My yoke upon you, and learn from Me, for I am gentle and humble in heart . . . ."

I am gentle and humble in heart," might best be summed up in the one word — unselfish. According to Jesus' testimony, that is the most Christlike attitude we can demonstrate. The attitude that releases joy and launches it from our lips is an attitude of unselfishness.

What does the Lord do to help broaden my horizons and assist me in seeing how selfish I am? Very simple: He gives me four busy kids who step on shoes, wrinkle clothes, spill milk, lick car windows, and drop sticky candy on the carpet.

You haven't lived until you've walked barefoot across the floor in the middle of the night and stomped down full force on a jack . . . or a couple of those little Lego landmines. I'll tell you, you learn real quick about your own level of selfishness.

Being unselfish in attitude strikes at the very core of our being. It means we are willing to forego our own comfort, our own preferences, our own schedule, our own desires for another's benefit. And that brings us back to Christ.

CHAPTER FIVE

*F*riends Make Life More Fun

When I look back across the landscape of my life, I am able to connect specific individuals to each crossroad and every milestone. A few of them have remained my friends to this very day. Each one has helped me clear a hurdle or handle a struggle, accomplish an objective or endure a trial—and ultimately laugh again.

I cannot even imagine where I would be today were it not for that handful of friends who have given me a heart full of joy. Let's face it, friends make life a lot more fun.

Laughter is definitely connected to staying involved with people. Stay involved! You will never regret it. Furthermore, it will help you grow up as you find yourself growing old. And the more involved you remain, the less concern you will have for how old you are.

When God is in our hearts of compassion, prompting us to get involved in helping others . . . when He is in our acts of generosity, honoring our support of those engaged in ministry . . . and when He is in our strong commitment, using our sacrifices to bless other lives, He does not forget us in our need. It is all so beautiful, so simple, so right. It is enough to make every one of us laugh out loud!

The bad news is: Ours is an arduous, long, and sometimes tedious journey through Cesspool Cosmos. And, observe, it is a walk, not a sprint.

The good news is: We are not alone on this demanding pilgrimage, which means that some folks we are traveling with make awfully good models to follow. So, follow them!

A large part of learning how to laugh again is being broad-shouldered enough to let things be . . . to leave room for differences . . . to applaud good results even if the way others arrive at them may not be our preferred method. It takes a lot of grace not to be petty, but, oh, the benefits!

To do otherwise is to clutter our minds with judgmental and borderline legalistic thoughts which become joy stealers. They rob us of a positive mind-set. And what happens then? We become petty, cranky, grim people who must have everyone poured into our mold before we are able to relax.

Agreeing on the same basics while encouraging each other to hang in there day after day is one of the many benefits of locking arms in close friendship with a small group of Christians. The group not only holds us accountable, but also reminds us we are not alone. I have found that I don't get as weary when I pull up close alongside a few like-minded brothers and take the time to cultivate a meaningful relationship.

Surely it is not blasphemous to think that laughter breaks out in heaven on special occasions. Why shouldn't it? There is every reason to believe that would happen in His infinite, holy presence, where all is well and no evil abides. After all, God sees everything that transpires in this human comedy of errors . . . He understands it all.

Y ou need me. I need you. Both of us need a few kindred spirits, people who understand us and encourage us. Both of us need friends who are willing to risk to help us and, yes, at times to rescue us. Friends like that make life more fun.

But all of us — you, me, *all of us* — need a Savior. . . . The everlasting relief He brings is enough to make us not only laugh again, but laugh forever.

CHAPTER SIX

*D*on't Forget to Have Fun as *Y*ou Grow Up

The longer I live the more I become convinced that our major battle in life is not with age but with maturity. Don't waste your time worrying about how old you are getting. Age is a matter of fact. Maturity, on the other hand, is a matter of choice.

God's specialty is bringing renewal to our strength, not reminders of our weakness. Take it by faith, He is well aware of your weaknesses; He just sovereignly chooses not to stop there. They become the platform upon which He does His best work.

But I rejoiced in the Lord greatly, that now at last you have revived your concern for me; indeed, you were concerned before, but you lacked opportunity."

Though getting up in years, Paul is rejoicing. Though without the comforts of home and the privileges of privacy, he is happy. Though he doesn't have a clue regarding his future, he is smiling at life. Though he is set aside, forced to stay in one place, completely removed from the excitement of a broader ministry, he is still rejoicing, still laughing. No matter what happened to him, Paul refused to be caught in the grip of pessimism.

N ot that I speak from want; for I have learned to be content in whatever circumstances I am."
Paul is contented.

To him it made no difference whether he was freed or bound to a soldier . . . whether the day was hot and humid or bleak and frigid . . . whether the Philippians sent a gift or failed to make contact. How wonderfully refreshing. How incredibly mature!

Some people are thermometers. They merely register what is around them. If the situation is tight and pressurized, they register tension and irritability. If it's stormy, they register worry and fear. If it's calm, quiet, and comfortable, they register relaxation and peacefulness.

Others, however, are thermostats. They regulate the atmosphere. They are the mature change-agents who never let the situation dictate to them.

CHAPTER SEVEN

*T*ake a Break . . .
to Laugh Again

At times we need to find relief from life's blistering winds of disappointment and discouragement. For me, nothing works better than a break in the schedule where hearty laughter and a whole change of pace takes my mind off the demands and deadlines.

We can choose joy regardless of our circumstances, our financial status, our occupation, our past failures, or our current distresses. Thank goodness, things don't have to be perfect or nearly perfect in order for us to focus on the bright side of life.

Virtually every day I can find at least one thing to laugh about. There may be a few exceptions, but those days are rare indeed. Even though pain or difficult circumstances may be our faithful companions, we encounter something each day that can prompt a chuckle or, for that matter, a hearty burst of laughter. And besides, it's healthy!

When our world begins to get too serious, we need momentary interruptions of just plain fun. A surprising day off, a long walk in the woods, a movie, an enjoyable evening relaxing with a friend over a bowl of popcorn, a game of racquetball or golf—these diversions can make all the difference in our ability to cope with life's crushing demands.

We need to give ourselves permission to enjoy various moments in life even though all of life is not in perfect order. This takes practice, but it's worth the effort.

S top reading only the grim sections of the newspaper. Watch less television and start reading more books that bring a smile instead of a frown. Locate a few acquaintances who will help you laugh more at life. Ideally, find Christian friends who see life through Christ's eyes, which is in itself more encouraging. Have fun together. Share funny stories with each other. Affirm one another.

We all look so much better and feel so much better when we laugh. I don't know of a more contagious sound. And yet there are so many who never weary of telling us, "Life is no laughing matter." It may not be for them, but I must tell you, it often is for me.

K nowing that God is causing "all things to work together for good," and remembering that we, His people, are on our way to an eternal home in the heavens without fears or tears, takes the sting out of this temporary parenthesis of time called earthly life.

What is your particular quest? For what are you leaning forward? There is something wonderfully exciting about reaching into the future with excited anticipation, and those who pursue new adventures through life stay younger, think better, and laugh louder!

The plan **is** progress, not perfection.
* The **past** is over, forget it.
* The **future** holds out hope, reach for it.

The plan is progress, not perfection.
- The past is over, forget it.
- The future holds out hope, reach for it.